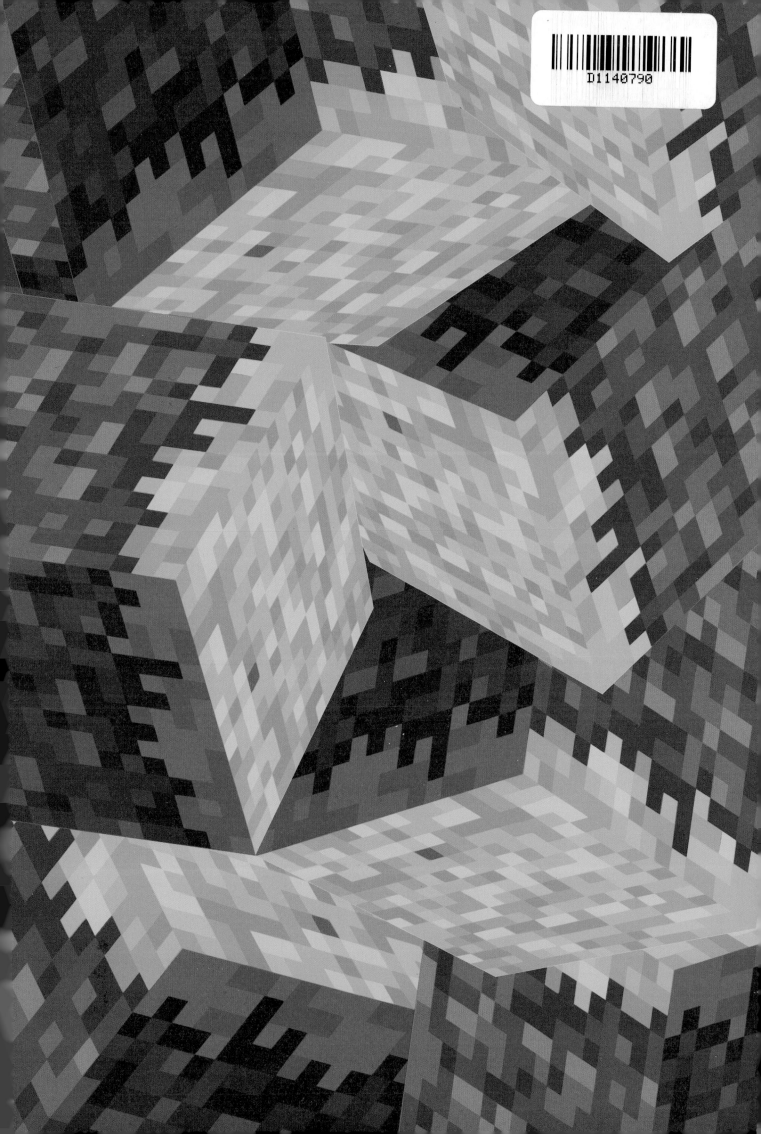

GamesMaster

PRESENTS

MINECRAFT

PS4 / XBOX ONE / Wii U / PC / PS3 / 360 / PS VITA / iOS / ANDROID

MINECRAFT'S CRAZIEST EASTER EGGS

26

6

Top 50 Minecraft Moments

Contents

10 EXCUSES TO KEEP PLAYING MINECRAFT

38

EVERY DODGE YOU NEED TO KEEP PLAYING YOUR FAVOURITE GAME!

A to Z MINECRAFT

70

Going back to school with the ABCs of Minecraft

Inside

TOP 50 MINECRAFT MOMENTS

From building your first house to Notch leaving Mojang, these are the 50 moments that define Minecraft

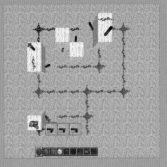

50

First time your house gets blown up by a creeper

Ooh golly, a creeper! Getting a bit close, isn't he? Uh oh, he's about to explode! I'll just escape into my carefully crafted new home. Oh... it's been destroyed. Darn.

49

Minecraft's many clones

FortressCraft? CraftWorld? Total Miner? The early 2010's saw a load of eerily familiar block-based sandboxes. Minecraft itself may have been heavily inspired by Infiniminer, but some of these similarities were startling.

48

Your first redstone circuit

Whether you're creating a trap or using Redstone circuits to trigger complicated events, there's a sense that you're toying with one of Minecraft's most powerful tools. Redstone circuits make game-makers of us all.

47

Your first death

Sooner or later, you get a little too adventurous. Maybe you strayed too far from your home base or were curious about that glowing orange stuff. Just remember, before beds, death was even more awful.

46

First Minecraft spin off – Story Mode

Minecraft: Story Mode takes the original game and turns it into an episodic adventure. The story follows a group searching out The Order of the Stone – four legendary adventurers who killed an ender dragon. Oh, and there's a pet pig!

45

Mojang's second game announced

Mojang's second game, Scrolls, was nothing like Minecraft. Instead, it was a card game where players would build decks of creatures and spells that they'd play against each other. Sadly, in June, 2015 Mojang said it would stop making new content for Scrolls. All together now, aaaah.

44

Minecraft: Pocket Edition revealed

Minecraft: Pocket Edition came to Windows, Android and Apple smartphones in 2011. It's a more stripped-down, Creative mode-focused version of the game compared to the original, but still offers a solid brick-breaking fix on the go. We like.

43 | Building your first hom

Minecraft's nights are dark and full of terro so before too long you'll need to build your first home. We'd suggest carving a cave int cliff face and walling yourself in for the nig won't be big, or pretty, but it will be yours.

42 | Reaching The End

Creating a path to The End requires you to mess with dark forces. As well as having to collect the eyes of endermen (bad enough), you then have to repair a glittering black portal. The sense of menace is overwhelming.

41

Minecraft EULA announcement

Who'd have thought some updated text could cause such an uproar? As servers started implementing microtransactions, Mojang issued a document that prevented server owners from charging for game-altering perks. The backlash from the confusion led to Notch tweeting: "Anyone want to buy my share of Mojang so I can move on with my life?"

40

The arrival of adventure maps

Before Mojang added support for Adventure Mode and command blocks, adventure maps worked on an honour system. A list of rules told you what you could and couldn't do – and usually asked you to not remove any blocks. Some even featured a story, told through separate text files.

39 | Killing the ender dragon

The monster gave Minecraft the crescendo moment it was lacking, and now few can forget the fear of seeing its huge dark form for the first time. Its ability to smash blocks make it a fearsome opponent for any player.

38

Rob McElhenney announced as the director for the upcoming Minecraft movie

Following the success of The LEGO Movie, Warner Brothers bought the film rights to Minecraft, which recently resurfaced after a few years in limbo. The fact that Rob McElhenney is directing is surprising, given he's best known for It's Always Sunny in Philadelphia, an excellent but very adult comedy.

Game over!

Score: 5

You cannot respawn in hardcore mod

Delete world

37 Hardcore mode introduced

Fancy something harder than hard mode? Say he to hardcore mode, in which when you die, you wo respawn. In fact, your game world will be deleted. Oh, and if you change your mind, bad luck: you ca switch the difficulty back.

Breeding animals 36

Nothing in Minecraft makes you feel as much like Doctor Frankenstein as breeding animals. Just get two of the same species beside one another and feed them both at the same time. They'll spawn an itty bitty baby animal. Aaah...

35

Herobrine Creepypasta created

It was only a matter of time before ghost stories started circulating online. The Creepypasta wiki preserves Minecraft's most famous one: a tale of a blank-eyed Minecraft man that lingers in the fog, stalking players and building strange totems.

34

Minecraft: Volume Alpha soundtrack is released

While you're busy gallivanting through the jungle biome, it's easy to forget that half the effect is a result of what's going into your earholes. But stop to think about it, and C418's gentle electronica is the perfect accompaniment to your blocky fun. The soundtrack, Volume Alpha, received a digital release back in 2011, but was also given a physical release – including a limited-edition run on transparent green vinyl.

33

Development of Cave Game

Cave Game was the very first Minecraft prototype, inspired by a blocky resource-gathering game called Infinmines. You can see an early build of Cave Game on YouTube here: http://bit.ly/1wIFNw3

32

Minecraft comes to consoles

Minecraft may have been available on PC since 2009, but its first console version didn't appear until 9 May, 2012, when it came to Xbox with split-screen multiplayer, and simpler crafting.

MAKE IT!
GROW YOUR OWN GRASS BLOCK!!!

Fancy making your own Minecraft grass block? Of course you do. And it's really pretty simple with our five step guide. Get growing!

YOU'LL NEED...

MATERIALS: Square flower pot; grass/cress/chive seeds, or a small plant (we used a chive plant); green and brown foam; felt-tip pens; scissors; double-sided sticky tape; ruler and pen

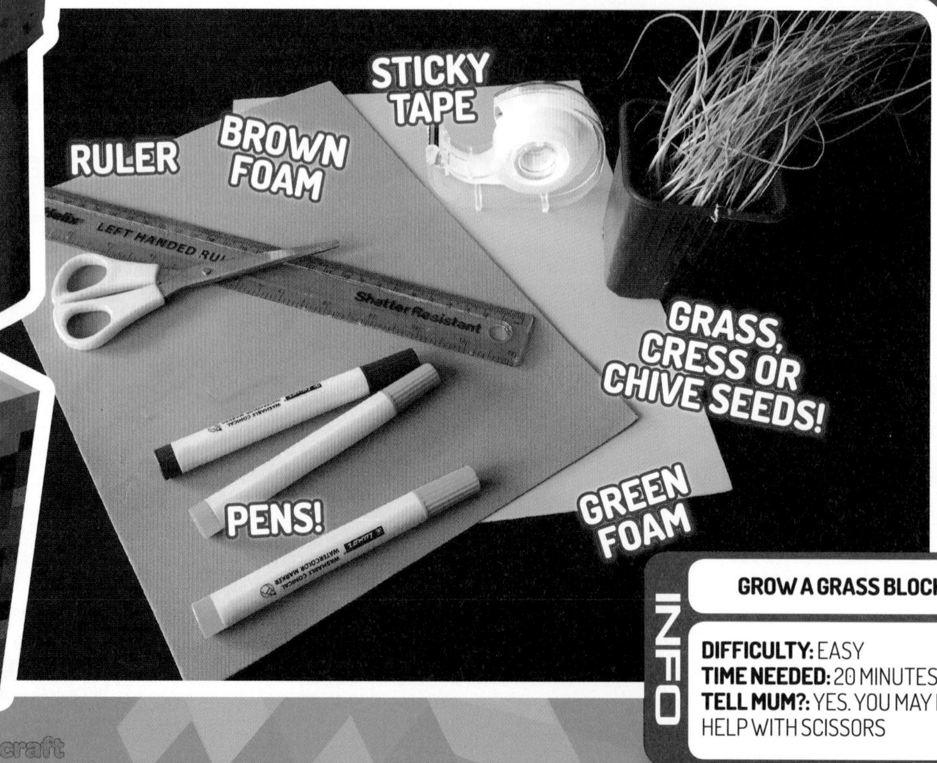

STICKY TAPE

RULER

BROWN FOAM

GRASS, CRESS OR CHIVE SEEDS!

PENS!

GREEN FOAM

THE HUMBLE GRASS BLOCK CAN BE YOURS TO LOVE IN REAL LIFE!

GROW A GRASS BLOCK!

INFO

DIFFICULTY: EASY
TIME NEEDED: 20 MINUTES
TELL MUM?: YES. YOU MAY NEED HELP WITH SCISSORS

1 MEASURE UP

Use a ruler to measure the width of your flowerpot
Add about half a centimetre to the overall measurement, in order to give space for the corners. Then, using a ruler, carefully measure out four panes of this width on the brown foam. It's also a good idea to leave a flap of a centimetre or two at one end. Make the panes almost the same height as your flowerpot.

USE YOUR RULER TO MEASURE YOUR FLOWERPOT

2 FOLD IT UP

Carefully cut out your sheet of brown foam, keeping the edges as straight as possible. Line up the ruler along each fold line, and use your scissors to score it - this will help you to make each fold as sharp as possible. Turn the foam over, and use a brown felt-tip to decorate the 'earth' section of your block. Don't bother making it too neat!

MAKE IT LOOK NICE AND EARTHY WITH YOUR PEN. IT'S A DIRTY JOB!

3 LOOK SHARP!

Turn the foam back over so that it's sat decoration-side down, and fold along your scored lines. Make sure you're folding them so that the decoration sits on the outside. If you're not used to using sharp scissors, get some help from an adult. We don't want any accidents!

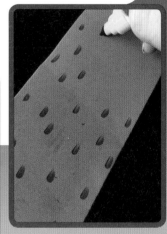

GET AN ADULT TO HELP YOU WITH THE SCISSORS

4 IN A FLAP...

Attach pieces of double-sided sticky tape to the reverse side of each pane, and then carefully stick it to your flowerpot, lining it up with the bottom edge. Start off with the small flap, so that it can be covered by the final pane.

5 TA–DA!

Repeat steps 1-4 using green foam, but this time with much smaller panes and using green felt-tip pens. Cut small notches along the bottom, attach with tape, then finally, fill your pot!

THE 10 BEST PETS IN MINECRAFT

Ordinary, exotic or extremely dangerous – why not try taming these ten incredible Minecraft pets!

It can be a lonely existence playing Minecraft. Whether you're building a glorious palace for yourself or just pottering about having a splendid adventure, it's always nicer to have other people with you. But when your friends aren't around, you don't have to ditch the pickaxe – get yourself a pet, and you'll never be alone again! You can share your adventures with Tweety, Fluffy or Mr Wuffles, or you can just keep them at home. The only thing is that of course, technically, there are only a limited amount of animals you can keep as 'pets', but we're choosing to bend the definition slightly and accept that all captured animals count. Yay variety!

PIG
Makin' bacon

In Minecraft, the humble pig is one of the easier animals to tame and domesticate, making him a great choice for the beginner who wants a little bit of oinky company. Firstly, lure your potential porky pal into an enclosed area with some carrots – this is where you'll be keeping him, so you can stick to the basics and build a little fenced-off pen, or you could go dramatic and build him a tiny pig-house. Once he's in the pen/pig-house, close it off so he can't escape, and voila! Your very own piggy friend.

CHICKEN
Feather Portal

So now you have your own pigs, you're looking to expand, right? Time to start turning your livestock collection into a farm with chickens. Like pigs, lure them into an enclosed area, but this time using wheat seeds, then block them in. Chickens give you eggs every five to ten minutes. Killing them gives you raw chicken, and killing them with fire gives you cooked chicken. Now we've got bacon and eggs sorted!

MOOSHROOM
Stew love it

You've got yourself some pigs and chickens and you're well on your way to starting a pretty decent farm. What else do farms need? Cows, probably. But you're bored of your garden-variety domesticated farmyard animals, so it's time to get a little more exciting. A mooshroom is a sort of cross between a regular cow and a mushroom, and the less you know about why that happened, the better. They're dappled red and white, with huge fungi all over their backs. Like regular cows, they can be milked with a bucket or killed to create leather and beef. However, shearing them will give you red mushrooms.

OCELOT
Cat's the way to do it

Wolves may be the dogs of the Minecraft world, but ocelots are the cats. In the wild, they appear as yellow and black-spotted cats, stalking chickens and scaring away creepers. They won't attack you, but they can sprint – so you'll have to be clever if you want to catch one. With an uncooked fish, wait for one to approach, then stay VERY still. They should follow you home and become your best friend.

WOLF
Howl Sanctuary

They might be fairly rare, and you might have to venture into the dark woods or the chilly tundra to find them, but a tamed wolf is the closest to man's best friend. Grab yourself a few bones to tame a wild wolf – each one has a one in three chance of taming the little guy, so keep trying if it doesn't work first time – and once you succeed, your new friend will get an orange collar and sit down before following you.

SILVERFISH
Small scales

The best thing about having silverfish as pets is that they're so tiny, you can have loads and they take up hardly any space. The first thing to remember is that they aren't actual fish, so don't make the mistake of building them a big watery tank only to find them drowned in the morning. You may recognise them from strongholds, where smashing a block that looks suspiciously like all the other stone blocks will spawn a wiggly little dude intent on destroying you. The best plan is to create a nice cage for them first – on creative mode, place a silverfish spawn block inside where you want them to be, and destroy it. They're the Minecraft equivalent of sea monkeys!

HORSE
Pony club

You'll find horses roaming the plains alongside donkeys, in 35 different colours. You can get brown, dark brown, even darker brown, black, grey, white, plus all of the above with various types of spots – whereas donkeys just come in your standard grey-brown. Sorry, donkeys. Unfortunately, horses are a bit trickier to tame than the animals we've seen so far, requiring you to mount them over and over again until the horse no longer bucks you off. Feeding them sugar and wheat will increase your chances, and a golden apple will also make a horse enter breeding mode. It's work, but you can put armour on horses, making them the coolest pet you can own.

ELDER GUARDIAN

Eye see you

If farmyard animals bore you, then maybe you're ready for the ultimate challenge – turning the elder guardian into your personal plaything. It looks like a cross between a really gross fish and a sea mine, and the secret to capturing this tricky beast is patience. You'll need to be invisible so it doesn't kill you, and you'll need loads of minecart tracks to push him towards his new prison. Also get milk, as your new pet has a habit of giving you mining fatigue.

SPIDER

World wide web

Nothing is more cuddly than an adorable spider, crawling all over your hands and face and into your mouth. No? Not a fan of spiders? Perhaps you'll still enjoy having them as pets, merely because a spider in a cage is a spider that's not in your mouth. You'll find them scuttling about anywhere that's dark, like caves, but darkness also makes them hostile, so be careful. Make sure it's nighttime, and lure the spider back to the little home. Once you've trapped him, make sure to close off the ceiling so he can't climb out...

ZOMBIE PIGMAN

Orc chops

Now we're getting really interesting. Who said all your pets had to be animals? Technically, the zombie pigman isn't really a human or an animal – he's a pigman, which makes him a bit of both, and therefore it's totally acceptable to keep him/it as a pet. Because Minecraft doesn't encourage the capture and keeping of monsters as pets, there's no real way to lure him - you'll just have to make him pursue you to his new prison.

STAMPY'S
TOP 10 TIPS

Polish your Minecraft skills with Stampy's handy tips

Chances are, if you're reading this, you know who Stampy is. You've watched his videos, shared his adventures, perhaps even bought his lovely book. But for anyone who doesn't play Minecraft, he's a bit of a mystery. Many folk could easily stroll past Stampy in the street, unaware they almost rubbed shoulders with a YouTube superstar; a man who gets more YouTube hits than many successful pop stars, with a legion of dedicated, block-bashing followers.

That's why the next few pages are dedicated to Stampy, whose real name is Joseph Garrett. We were lucky enough to interview him, and naturally we asked him for all his closely-guarded YouTube secrets.

His top ten tips are a smashing place to start if you need some help from an expert.

STAMPY FACTS

He's one of YouTube's biggest stars, but how much do we really know about Stampy? Well, rather a lot, actually. Here's a list of some fascinating Stampy tidbits.

1 Sleep tight. On your first night, make a bed. You don't want to be out in the dark when the googlies spawn.

2 Make sure you always use the right tool. Start by making a wooden pickaxe so you can gather cobblestone, then make stone tools. With iron, use an iron pickaxe to mine diamonds.

3 Don't get lost. Create a map and make a note of where your house is. When exploring a cave leave a trail of torches behind you so you can follow them to get back out.

4 The easiest way to get food at first is meat. Once you have a house, making a wheat farm should be a top priority. Eventually plant carrots and potatoes.

01 Stampy's channel is one of the fastest growing channels of ANY genre.

02 His daily YouTube views are, on average, over four million every single day!

03 Stampy uploads new videos every day. It looks fun, but it's a lot of work.

04 In December 2013, Stampy's channel was temporarily terminated by Google. Still no idea why!

5

5 Protect your house from googlies. Keeping the area around your house bright is very important. The googlies only spawn when it's dark. You could also dig a pit around your base that the googlies can't jump over. Setting up traps can also be helpful, just be careful not to get caught in them yourself.

6 Diamonds are probably the most precious and useful item in the game. It is much easier to find them when in a natural cave but is safer to find them digging in a straight line.

7

7 Lots of people are scared to learn how redstone works, but try experimenting by making a doorbell or piston.

"I think people mainly enjoy the humour and stories I tell in my videos"

05 Stampy first started out recording amusing real-life skits, & animation.

06 Joseph studied video production at college and uni.

07 His first videos were actually for games like Call of Duty and Halo.

08 Before YouTube, Joseph was a barman. He left his job to do videos.

09 He's doing amazingly well now, but Joseph started out filming in his bedroom .

> "It's a lot more fun to put all your energy into making great videos."

8 Get creative. You can get bored of playing Minecraft if you don't have an idea for something to build. If you don't know what to build, try building your house or school. Building giant versions of your favourite characters is fun too. If you still don't know what to build, try watching one of my videos and try re-building what I build but do it in your own style.

9 **Play with friends. Minecraft can get lonely when playing by yourself. Inviting friends can make it lots more fun.**

10 Defeating the Ender Dragon is one of the toughest challenges. Before entering The End make sure you are 100% prepared. Bring lots of food and equipment. You want at least a full set of iron armour but diamond is better. You want a bow and LOTS of arrows. A pumpkin on your head means that the Endermen won't attack you first.

STAMPY'S LOVELY BOOK

Lovely puzzles, games, comic strips, video tips, secrets and !

Stampy's Lovely Book is Joseph Garrett's first official book, and it's available from Egmont Publishing for £7.99

---

10 Joseph met his buddy iBallisticSquid in January 2013. The rest is history...

11 Joseph's parents were happy for him to live rent-free until he made his channel.

12 The logo on Joseph's channel, was designed by his father. Awesome!

13 Stampy gets well over 3,000 messages a day. That's a lot of mail.

I'LL MESS YOU UP BIGTIME!!!

INCREDIBLE...

ENDER DRAGON FACTS!

Everything you need to know about Minecraft's favourite boss

BRAINIAC!
The Ender Dragon was the first 'final' boss in Minecraft, but now that honour goes to the Wither which is an even tougher fight. But the Ender Dragon will always be extra special to us!

EGG-CELLENT!

You will only ever get a Dragon Egg from the very first time you beat the Ender Dragon which makes it the rarest item on any given map. It'll also grant you the ability to teleport up to seven spaces away – a bit like Endermen. It'll be incredibly handy to use if you ever need to escape a troubling situation.

I'M NOT ALL BAD!

PUMPKIN!

If you wear a pumpkin on your head instead of a helmet you won't make the Endermen angry and can just concentrate on the dragon. You won't be able to see as well as you normally would – but it's better than being harassed by loads of Endermen while trying to fight.

DON'T TRY SCRAMBLING THIS EGG

ORANGE YOU GLAD TO SEE ME?!

DYNAMITE!

The Ender Dragon recharges its health using Ender Crystals. When these explode they are 50% more powerful than TNT. If you've got a bow and arrow you can shoot these while the Ender Dragon is recharging to do loads of damage at once. It's a great tactic to help you take it down even faster.

TAKE OUT THESE CRYSTALS

RECHARGE YOUR HEALTH ALL YOU WANT, WE'RE STILL GOING TO BEAT YOU!

BAD BREATH!

Minecraft's 1.9 update means that the Ender Dragon's breath now shoots further, it can hurt you with its wings and no longer takes damage from snowballs, so it's an even bigger challenge now.

ENDER GAME

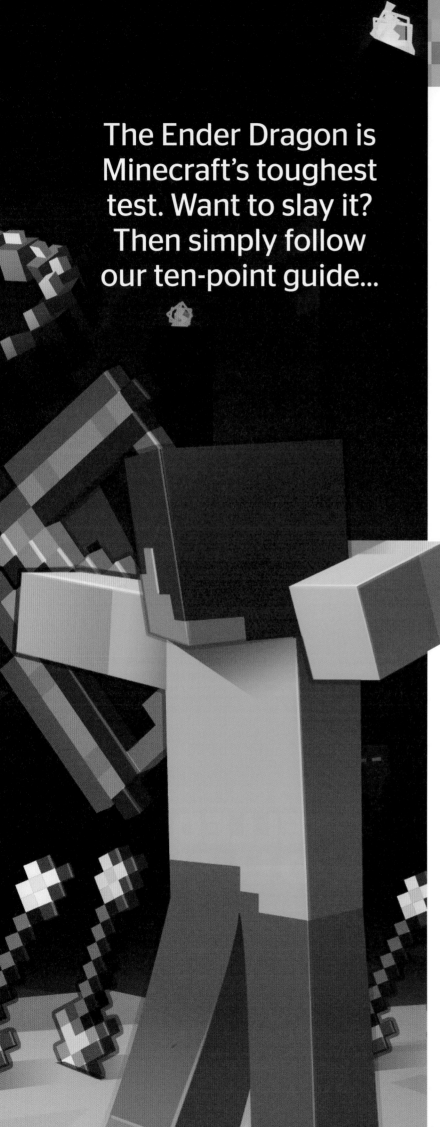

The Ender Dragon is Minecraft's toughest test. Want to slay it? Then simply follow our ten-point guide...

1 BEFORE YOU GO

Once you reach The End, there's no going back until you've defeated the Ender Dragon. You'll need enchanted weapons and armour, strength and health potions, some cheap building materials, and a *lot* of arrows.

2 FINDING THE STRONGHOLD

You need at least 12 eyes of ender – crafted with an ender pearl and blaze powder. Throw an eye into the air and it'll float before hitting the floor: the direction it floats is the direction in which you'll need to travel to reach the stronghold.

3 END PORTAL

Head to the stronghold and search for the end portal. You'll find it toward the bottom, suspended over a pool of lava and protected by a silverfish spawner. Pop your ender eyes into each slot of the portal and it'll activate.

4 THE END

Take care when you enter: you spawn on a small obsidian platform, under or beside the main End island. Dig your way to the top or build a platform across. The Ender Dragon *shouldn't* attack until you reach the surface.

5 DEALING WITH ENDERMEN

The End is teeming with endermen, and they can make a would-be dragonslayer's life hell. Pumpkin hats waste a valuable armour slot, so dump a water bucket on the ground near to a group to de-aggro them.

6 SOMEWHERE TO HIDE

You may find that your first scuffle with The End's draconian dictator doesn't go quite as planned. So make sure you dig a nice safe area to fall back to with healing items and enough supplies to repair your gear.

7 HEALING CRYSTALS

Each main obsidian pillar contains an ender crystal. They're your first target. Their purple rays heal the Ender Dragon, so killing him while they're active is impossible. Luckily, they're fragile. A few well-aimed arrows should do it.

8 CAGED CRYSTALS

Two crystals are sneakily encased behind iron bars, stopping you from taking them out at range. So you can jump-stack your way to the top of a pillar and find that you can easily knock down the barrier.

6 ACID ATTACK

The Ender Dragon has two attacks. His long-range acid ball is easy to avoid and — if you're wearing enchanted armour — not too harmful. His second, an acid spray, is much more deadly. So keep moving and dodging.

10 FINISH HIM

After circling the pillars a few times, the Ender Dragon will stop and hover over the centre of the island. Now's your chance to pelt him with arrows! A purple explosion will eventually signal your victory.

MINECRAFT'S CRAZIEST EASTER EGGS

Rainbow sheep and killer bunnies? You've got to be yolking

Easter is, as everybody knows, a most sacred time of year. Easter is about sacrifice. It's about rebirth. It's about the holy ritual of shoving novelty chocolate into your face-hole until your sweat whatever it is they put in Creme Eggs (paradise goo? Liquid unicorn? Best not to ask).

Of course, we want to talk about easter eggs - and by that we mean hidden secrets, not actual eggs - and Minecraft's got loads of them stuffed inside it.

But like all good things in Minecraft, they're buried underneath the surface, revealing their delicious mysteries to only the most persistent pickaxes...

We've dug through every crevice of code to bring you Minecraft's super-secret treats. And what did we find on our easter egg hunt? Upside-down animals! Encrypted puzzles! Spelling errors! Barefaced lies! Other things you probably don't want to put in your mouth! And most of all, hilarious hacks that remind us why Minecraft is so sweet.

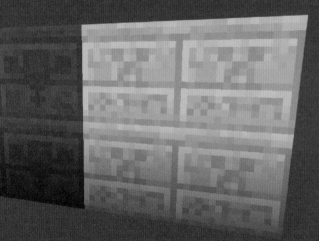

01

CHISELLED GOOD LUCKS

Grab a chunk of chiseled sandstone in your blocky hands (it's two sandstone slabs stacked on top of each other), and take a squiz at it. Check out those two shady little blobs right in the middle. Yup, that's a creeper face. And if that wasn't suspicious enough for you, chiseled red sandstone is quite clearly harbouring the spooky, three-skulled shadow of the wither. Now you can rest easy in the knowledge that your empire is built from the petrified corpses of your enemies.

02 | LOADING WITH A CHANCE OF MEAT-BOATS

Okay, so the sweet stuff isn't for everyone. Fortunately, there is a savoury easter egg hidden deep within Minecraft's code. So deep, in fact, that this particular menu screen mishap only has a 0.01% chance of floating to the surface every time you boot up the game. Even though it's spelled out in huge cobblestone letters, only the keenest of peepers will notice the game's title appearing as the jumbled-up "MINCERAFT" once in a blue moon.

03

OUT OF THEIR GOURDS

Each Hallowe'en, many skellybobs, zombies and creepers hide their heads inside pumpkins and jack o'lanterns for the night. This easter egg isn't just adorably spooky – it can actually be very useful if you're well-prepared for October 31st. Upgrade a tool with a Looting enchantment, get cracking those scary skulls, and you'll find that the veggie visors will plop right off enemy heads and into your inventory.

04

STEVE-IL TWIN

You haven't heard of Steve's evil twin? Oh boy. Turns out the creepy tale is totally untrue, and there's no source code that would ever spawn something like Herobrine. That hasn't stopped Mojang from fuelling our nightmares, however – the milky-eyed one has repeatedly popped up in official art, and is referenced in every set of patch notes. What's going on?!

05 | ALPHABET GET!

Those odd little symbols that whizz about the table when you're riffling through your bumper book of enchantments don't half look mysterious and impressive. But they're far from random squiggles: they're actually part of the Standard Galactic Alphabet. Each symbol corresponds to one of the 26 letters of the alphabet, meaning it's possible to decipher coded words in the enchantments you perform. Uselessly interesting.

06

CORE BLIMEY

One of Minecraft's most discussed secrets is what exactly Papa Minecraft's character drops upon meeting a sticky end in the servers. Rumour has it that somewhere, buried in the game's code, is a command that produces a single, shiny red apple once a player manages to slay digi-Notch. If it was once true, we don't reckon it is any more. Sad…

07

RABID RABBIT

It just wouldn't be Easter without fluffy bunnies. Sorry, did we say "fluffy"? We meant "killer". Killer bunnies. Your diamond armour has no power here. The Killer Bunny used to be a rare natural spawn, but you'll need a command block to summon one now. We'd recommend extreme caution as they've got a vicious streak a mile wide.

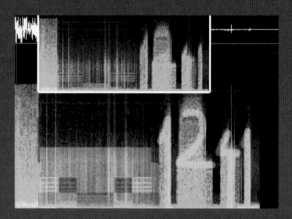

08

WHAT'S IN A NAME?

Renaming Minecraft's animals changes their very DNA. Hunt down a name tag, whip up an anvil and gather your motley crew of critters. Dubbing a humble sheep "jeb_" will cause it to turn into Disco Sheep. Name any mob "Dinnerbone" or "Grumm", and they'll instantly be flipped upside-down.

09

FACE IN THE MUSIC

Getting to the bottom of this mystery requires diamond-hard determination. For starters, you've got to get hold of a rare music disc – Music Disc 11. That's the strange, broken-looking one. Root around in your game's Minecraft folders and grab the disc's .ogg file. Next, run it through spectrogram software to reveal… well, just look at it. It doesn't take much to spot the Minecraft-esque face and the numbers 1241. What does it mean? We don't have a Scooby Doo.

10
HACK 'N' SPLASH

On logging into the game, you're always greeted by a "splash" slapped over the game's title – a sunny yellow message in Minecraft's pixelated font. Firing up the game on 1st June prompts the "Happy birthday, Notch!" to appear. Uncover a Pokemon reference by dipping into your Minecraft folders and deleting the one named splash.txt, making sure not to delete META-INF before that. The splash changes to "missingno" – the glitch species of Pokemon found in the first gen of the JRPG.

11
MOJANGLED BANNER

This secret crafting recipe will have you tearing down your ugly drapes and plastering Mojang's logo all over the show. Rustle up your standard banner out of six blocks of wool and a stick. Next, get an enchanted golden apple. Mashing the two together in a crafting grid will create a snazzy Mojang banner: you can even include dye to match your potted plants! You can't put a price on good taste!

12
FAR, FAR AWAY

Not The End – but the real end of the Minecraft world, known as the Far Lands, where horrors far greater than angsty dragons rear their glitchy heads. Layers of ground and sky stack and float in between each other, and the secret borderlands are so broken that it's not your character who's moving around – the ground is moving underneath you. Surely just legend?!

31

Minecraft reaches 100 million registered users

On 25 February 2014, Notch tweeted to announce that Minecraft had reached a staggering 100 million users, adding that 14 million of those players had paid for the full version. The figure is a testament to Minecraft's global appeal, and cements Minecraft's place as one of the biggest games in the world today. Minecraft's playerbase has only grown since, and more than 20 million players have bought the game.

30

Baking your first cake

Baking your first cake in Minecraft is less about nutritional value and more about the gesture. This isn't survival: this is making both your mum and Mary Berry proud. Look at you, welcoming guests in a traditional fashion!

29

Minecraft Classic changes with the times

The first Minecraft, now referred to as Minecraft Classic, arrived in 2009. It contained an early version of survival mode which gave you points for killing mobs.

28 Crafting your first tools

Whether you first opt for a pick, a shovel or an axe, your first set of tools is what separates Minecraft man from mob. Sure, they're probably made of wood and will give you splinters when you use them, but it's better than clawing at trees with your hands!

27

Official Minecraft trailer passes 130 million views

"Let's go to a place where everything is made of blocks, where the only limit is your imagination." The first few lines of the official Minecraft trailer captures the magic of the game perfectly.

26

Taming a wolf

Unless your name is Mowgli, wolves aren't inclined to be too friendly. Unless, that is, you tame them. Feed a wolf a bone and there's a one in three chance that it will become your faithful friend, and attack your enemies.

25 New-gen versions of Minecraft released

Minecraft scaled beautifully to the demands of phones and iPads, but its 2014 release on PlayStation 4 and Xbox One gave it the power of a new generation of hardware to play with. Split-screen multiplayer was a fantastic addition.

24

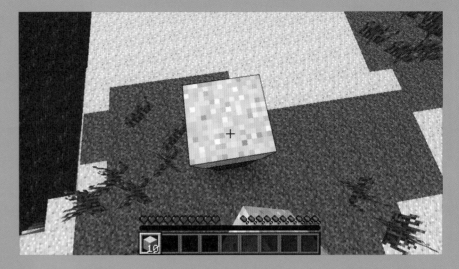

First LEGO Minecraft set

Minecraft and LEGO were always meant to be together. The final sets let you build forts in different biomes, and a plastic replica of the ender dragon that's far too cute to be scary.

23 | ## Your first nerd pole

Need a beacon to guide you home after an adventurous jaunt? That's why you need a nerd pole, my friend – and your first one marks your debut as a serious explorer. Put simply, it's a really, really tall pile of blocks: just keep jumping and placing a new block under your feet each time.

21

Minecraft on stage at Gamescom

In August 2013, Sony announced that it had secured Minecraft as a launch title for PS4. It was a huge show of faith for an indie title (albeit an already hugely successful one).

22 | ## First diamond pickaxe

You can spend hours, even days, searching for your first diamond ore block. But it's worth the effort, as when you've finally harvested enough you can craft a diamond pick. It digs through materials at lightning speed, and seems to last forever.

20

Hololens demo

Welcome to the future. This was Microsoft's message when it used Minecraft to show off the capabilities of its HoloLens augmented-reality headset – and it's well worth watching on YouTube. This is Minecraft spread across the surfaces of your living room's three dimensions. Please be real!

19

Surviving the first night

When the sun sets on your first day in Minecraft you'll discover just how dark the game can be. Creepers, zombies and spiders will prey on you till the dawn comes to burn them away. Fear the night!

18

First Minecraft mods

Believe it or not, installing Minecraft mods was once even more of a hassle. The mods were simpler, too. Instead of complex modpacks full of tools, blocks and machines, they were small tweaks and additions to improve the then limited game.

17

Entering the nether

The Minecraft alpha 1.2 Halloween update brought a molten underworld to Minecraft. Notch introduced this burning hellscape as a means of fast travel – one step in the nether is the equivalent of eight overground – but really it was a new level of challenge. The unique blocks and treasure hidden in the underworld made it a tempting target for raiders, but the underworld fortresses hid hordes of enemies, and it's all-too-easy to fall into the lakes of lava.

16

Redstone update

The Redstone update gave us blocks that increased the complexity of builds. Daylight sensors, pressure plates, trapped chests and more resulted in more ambitious Redstone circuits.

15 | Multiplayer mode

Alpha 1.0.15 launched survival multiplayer servers in August 2010, but it wasn't until the release of the Xbox 360 game in 2012 that split screen multiplayer arrived. Finally, someone to hold your hand at night!

Edit Server Info

Server Name

Our Minecraft Server

Server Address

ourmcserver.dyndns.org_

Done

Cancel

12

Horse update

The Horse update added horses and donkeys that you could tame and ride. Suddenly you could find saddles and even armour for your steeds. So why the long face?!

13

First online servers

Popular servers attract hundreds of players at a time. The world record for the most people in a Minecraft world at one time is 2,622!

14

Default female character

Steve is great! Practical, dependable chap that he is, he's your man in the game world, doing all the work for you. Except, he doesn't represent 50% of the world's population. Meet Alex, AKA the red-ponytailed lady Steve. Introduced as an option on PC in September 2014 and on console in April 2015, she's the female default character, and every bit as cool as her blocky brother.

11 | Update that changed the world

It's easy to take the variety of Minecraft's worlds for granted now, but before the 1.7.2 update, things were much plainer. The so-called "update that changed the world" added 11 new biomes: from savannahs to oceans.

HOW TO DRAW MINECRAFT PIGS!

Pen perfect porkers using our pink piggy pattern!

WANT to draw Minecraft's perky porkers? Well, there's snout to it, if you use our grid to guide you. Just follow the pattern above, making sure you focus on what's in each square. You'll have perfected our piggies before you can say 'sausages'!

OINK, OINK!

JUST COPY THE PATTERN ABOVE, GOING SQUARE BY SQUARE. SIMPLE!

GREY HAVENS

THE Elven city of Grey Havens has been the most difficult area to build. It's the city that the fellowship sail from at the end of The Return of the King.

STAR BUILD!

OUR FAVOURITE

COOL BUILDS!

Ardacraft are building Tolkein's Middle-earth - and it looks amazing!

SHIRELY NOT?!

FROM Bag End and Hobbiton to The Prancing Pony and Bucklebury Ferry, all of The Lord of the Rings' landmarks feature in this incredible build.

ARDACRAFT

THE team behind this amazing build is led by founder Jack Ashbridge. The team started with 25 builders, but has now increased as the project has grown.

WHICH WAY TO THE SHIRE?

10 EXCUSES TO KEEP PLAYING MINECRAFT

We've all been there. You're just putting the finishing touches on your majestic castle when your boss/teacher/passengers nag you to stop playing Minecraft, for silly reasons like 'eating' and 'sleeping' and 'homework'. Next time it happens use one of these excuses!

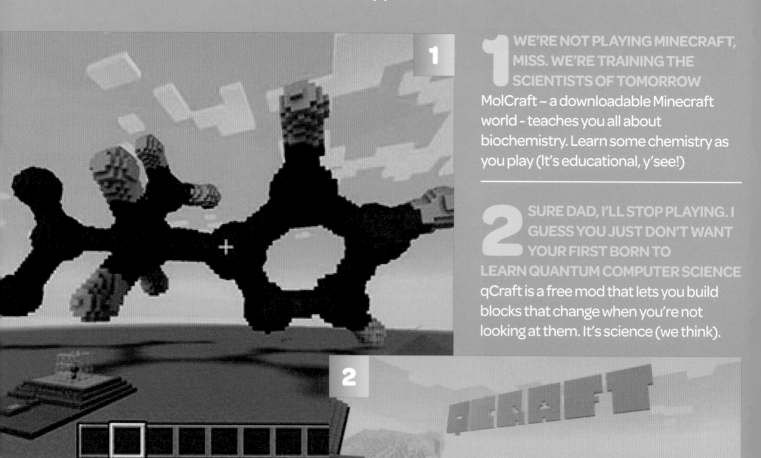

1 WE'RE NOT PLAYING MINECRAFT, MISS. WE'RE TRAINING THE SCIENTISTS OF TOMORROW

MolCraft – a downloadable Minecraft world - teaches you all about biochemistry. Learn some chemistry as you play (It's educational, y'see!)

2 SURE DAD, I'LL STOP PLAYING. I GUESS YOU JUST DON'T WANT YOUR FIRST BORN TO LEARN QUANTUM COMPUTER SCIENCE

qCraft is a free mod that lets you build blocks that change when you're not looking at them. It's science (we think).

3

IF I STOP PLAYING MINECRAFT, CAN I WATCH A MOVIE INSTEAD?

Not just any movie – the original Star Wars remade in Minecraft! No sound, but you can hum the music and do your own voices. Bet you do a mean Chewbacca…

4

GO TO THE THEATRE? BUT WITH MINECRAFT, I'M ALREADY THERE!

Show anti-gaming parents this excellent recreation of the Globe Theatre – the stomping ground of that William Shakespeare dude. No parent could accuse you of mindless gaming when you're learning about the Bard.

5

MINECRAFT IS TEACHING ME TO COMPUTER CODE. LEAVE ME ALONE, OR I'LL BLOCK YOU FROM THE INTERNET FOREVER

We all use computers, but how do our favourite apps and games work? Download LearnToMod and you can play Minecraft AND learn to code at the same time.

6 GO TO AN ART GALLERY? FOOLISH PARENTS, MINECRAFT LETS ME LIVE IN ART

Ever dreamed of climbing inside your favourite paintings and having a wander about? Tate Worlds are a series of free maps wherein you can explore worlds based on famous art.

7 NO I CAN'T PLAY OUTSIDE, I'M TRAVELLING THE WORLD

This is no idle get out. Take a stroll through several Minecraft mods and you could tick off the entire Seven Wonders Of The World by lunchtime. Mount Rushmore, the Eiffel Tower, all of Denmark – just a few mouse clicks away.

8 I'M NOT PLAYING A GAME, I'M TRAINING TO BECOME A TOWN PLANNER

A staff member of the City of Ottawa took the city's open data and created GeoOttaWOW – giving users access to faithful recreations of roads, streets and landmarks of Canada's capital. They hope it will inspire young people to develop an interest in city planning. That's what our giant zombie pit is – the future of Canadian infrastructure.

9

9 I WASN'T PLAYING MINECRAFT, I WAS CRAFTING THE ULTIMATE ROMANTIC GESTURE

Show your special someone that you love them nearly as much as Minecraft with this heartwarming 'I LUV U' message. If they ask why you sculpted it from dirt, laugh in their face (romantically) and explain that you need the diamonds for more important crafting projects. Get rejected, and you get more alone time with Minecraft. That's a win-win!

10

10 'PLAYING' MINECRAFT? HOW DARE YOU! I'M MAKING US RICH

Brandon Relph, 15, owns a business helping clients build whatever they want created in Minecraft. He's already made over £10,000. So get your boss or teacher off your back by explaining you're on the verge of the next million dollar Minecraft idea. Maybe they'll invest too?

Build your ideal island getaway!... in Minecraft!

POST | CARD

SUMMER LOVIN'

The summer holidays are finally upon us – hooray! Time for some well-deserved sun, sea and sand. But no matter where you're going away this summer, a week or two just won't be long enough, so let's get some inspiration and make our own digital beach resort...

1

PICK YOUR LOCATION

YOU KNOW what they say: location, location, location! You'll want to find a **decent-sized patch** of sand for your **beach resort**, and then level it off so that you've got a flat space to work with.

2

FENCE IT OFF

NOBODY wants their holiday interrupted by stray wildlife, so it's worth building a **fence** around the back edge of your resort to keep out the riff-raff. **Creepers not welcome here!**

3

LAY YOUR FOUNDATIONS

BUILD yourself a **beach hut** for a true summer feel. Start with the base – we went for an 8x9 platform held up on four stilts over the sea for great views across the water.

4

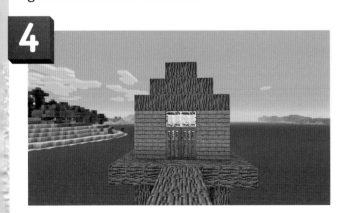

BUILD YOUR HUT

FOR a really 'beachy' look, the best material is wood, so pick a shade you like and go crazy! Ours is 5x7 blocks. You also might want some **big windows,** for admiring the view...

INSPIRATION

ADD A THEME PARK – we really want to go on the rides of Enmah's build!

RENT AN APARTMENT – Melany23's build feels like a realistic holiday option.

TRY A VILLA – We're jealous of the pool in SkyrimThomas's build.

5

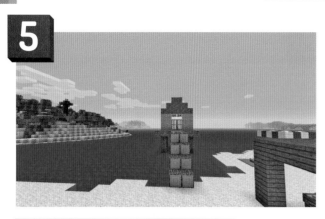

5. JOIN IT UP WITH A PIER

WHAT'S the use of a **beach hut** if nobody can reach it? Build a pier two blocks wide from your hut back to the shore, to act as a **bridge.** Be sure to add some steps to climb up.

6

6. MAKE UMBRELLAS

YOU'LL need some shade to **lounge** around in, so create a **parasol** or two. Use wooden blocks to build the stick, then blocks of coloured wool to form the **canopy**.

7

7. ADD SUN LOUNGERS

TO MAKE some comfy seats, just place a line of three **wooden blocks**, and then place a slab of the same wood at the top end. Repeat to make as many loungers as you like for lazing in the sun.

8

8. PROVIDE A PICNIC BLANKET

IT WOULD be rude not to provide **snacks** for your guests (being on holiday is hungry work) so lay out some squares of carpet to form a picnic blanket and scatter it with treats. **Cake is a must!**

9

9. DIG YOUR POOL

IF YOU want somewhere other than the sea to swim, it's time to dig a **pool**. Use buckets of water to fill it, but we'd recommend getting the digging finished first!

10

10. ADD SOME FLOURISHES

TO MAKE your pool a bit more exciting, why not add a few **extra touches?** You can build some steps into the **pool**, or even use wooden blocks and slabs to make a diving board.

11

11. SLIDE IN

ADD a **slide** by building a set of one-block steps beside your pool. Build up another set of steps on either side, one block higher than the **middle set** – so it forms a channel going down.

12

12. LET IT FLOW

PUT a ladder at the back and climb to the top, then empty a **bucket of water** towards the pool. It should flow down the channel you've made, giving you an impromptu waterslide.

13

13. BUILD YOUR BEACH BAR

IN CASE thirst strikes, build a **beach bar** out of wooden blocks, with some wooden slabs beside it for stools. We added a **brewing stand** to ours so we can whip up some fancy drinks.

INSPIRATION

OPEN AT NIGHT – Take advice from Aphobis' build and add some fancy lighting.

ADD MORE HUTS – Makaramoto's build looks really peaceful with all those huts.

BY THE BAY – We like the seats right on the shore in Kingsnakexxx's build.

14

14. ADD SOME SHADE AND TORCHES

YOU DON'T want any drinks getting hot, but it's easy to build some **shade** over your bar – just make sure you leave the sides open! Add **torches** to stop it getting too dark.

HUNGRY? GET HARVESTCRAFT!

Amazing!

Cook cheeseburgers and cake in minecraft's tastiest mod! It's all about learning to live off of the land – here's what you can get up to...

NOM NOM!

Grow tons of **new ingredients** to cook with. Plant peppers, lettuce, parsnips, onions, rhubarb, tomatoes... You can even grow cotton to make string!

FRUIT 'N' VEG! TASTIC!

Fruit trees aren't just colourful – they're delicious, too. The fruit grows back, and you can combine saplings and fruit to plant more trees for your own orchard.

MIND YOUR BEESWAX

Beehives appear in trees. Break one to get a queen bee, which can make honey and beeswax by placing it in an apiary (those white bee hive boxes you sometimes see). Then you can use that to craft candles!

CHEF TASTIC!

Here's the best bit – mega-yummy food. Try making cheeseburgers, pizza, sushi, full English breakfasts, glazed hams and even rainbow-coloured 'epic bacon'.

SWEET TOOTH

Everybody loves dessert, and there's loads to choose from now. Chocolate sprinkles cake, maybe? What about a doughnut, or gummy bears? We want to eat them all!

JUICE BAR

Got a pressing need for some juice? Use the new presser to turn lemons into lemonade and squeeze OJ from oranges.

WELL WELL WELL

Forget about hunting for lakes: now you can keep an infinite source of water in your home with sinks. Brick wells look great outdoors.

HOW TO INSTALL HARVESTCRAFT

First, go to files.minecraftforge.net to download Forge Modloader for your PC or Mac. Click the fle to install. Then, grab Pam's HarvestCraft here: http://bit.ly/1VwPyyz (check the version of HarvestCraft matches your version of Forge). Drag the downloaded file into the mods folder of your game's Minecraft folder, and start playing!

QUICK BUILD!

Make a fancy looking bridge in under 5 minutes!

5 MINUTES!

START HERE!

1 START by building a basic bridge shape with the stone bricks – layered steps at the edges and flat at the top.

2 NOW start adding your stairs to the edges of the blocks to make the bridge easier to walk over and to make it look nicer.

3 ADD stone brick borders to the steps and a few stone brick stairs under the bridge to give it a rounder edge.

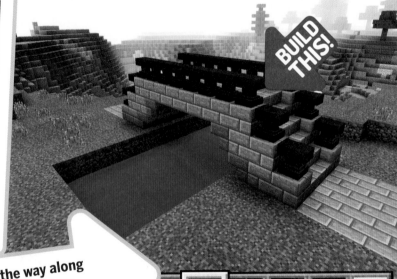

BUILD THIS!

4 NOW add anvils all the way along the top to look like a fancy iron fence border and you're done!

HOW MANY ZOMBIE VILLAGERS CAN YOU SPOT?

It's a zombie-fest! But how many can you spot below?

ZOMBIE VILLAGER...

SEE HOW MANY YOU CAN SPOT IN THIS LOT

IF there's anything worse than a moaning, stumbling zombie, it's an entire screen-full of them! We've packed the frame above with your green-headed friends. But just how many have we been able to cram in? Write your answer down!

YAY! I DID IT! I COUNTED:

ZOMBIE VILLAGERS

WRITE YOUR ANSWER HERE...

BEST GAMES CREATED IN MINECRAFT

Rabid gameplayer? You need never leave the comfort of your own blocky universe again...

Super Mario Maker

You could say that Super Mario Maker owes more of a debt to Minecraft than the other way around. Turn Minecraft into a cheerful, challenging platformer

Super Mario Brothers

http://bit.ly/1DEwCDi

Mario's blocky world is perfectly suited to Minecraft, as this charming Super Mario Mod demonstrates. This funtime little mod captures both the sights and the sounds of the Super Mario universe with a suite of custom blocks representing warp pipes, brick walkways and the famous floating question-mark loot blocks. It's almost like a Nintendo-flavoured home from home.

You can break these blocks by jumping and hitting them with your super hard Super Mario head – just like in, erm, real life –

all while clothed in Mario's stylish red cap and blue pants combo. Treasure blocks will even make a satisfying ping when you hit them, and there are classic Mario noises for jumping and hitting a flagpole, which rewards you with that familiar Mario fanfare.

The blocks and items are all craftable in survival mode, but this mod is great for making your own courses in creative mode, where you can arrange the brick blocks and warp pipes into great jumping courses in a few minutes. It's like a dream made real, that's what this is.

This mod requires Forge to work, which you can download here http://bit.ly/1IWLVHN.

Oh my days, this is making our heads pop just thinking about it. Make and mould your own fantasy Mario worlds!

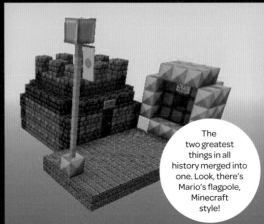

The two greatest things in all history merged into one. Look, there's Mario's flagpole, Minecraft style!

Assassin's Creed

Every year the Assassin's Creed series gives us a new city or two to explore with magic assassin parkour skills. Anything the Assassins can do Minecraft can do too, as you'll see…

Assassin Craft

http://bit.ly/1SQ9FmG

The iconic garb of the Assassins can easily be yours in Minecraft thanks to the Assassin Craft mod. This adds a bunch of new recipes that bring the killer cowls and weapons of the series into your Minecraft world, from Arno's French cutlass to Altair's signature flowing white robes.

The mod also adds Assassin's Creed guards and villains to dispatch with a variety of crossbows and hidden blades. There's a blacksmith to help you gear up, and the Romulus dungeon, full of enemies and secret treasure. The cutest addition is the hay bale block, which you can dive onto from any height to avoid taking falling damage. You'll finally be able to perform the leap of faith in Minecraft!

Roman City

http://bit.ly/21RAYDb

The great thing about Minecraft is that you can visit almost any city that has featured in an Assassin's Creed game. Want to recreate Unity? Try the 1:1 recreation of Paris in Minecraft (http://bit.ly/1jQeeB5). Prefer Syndicate? Try the London map instead (http://bit.ly/1SQ59o3).

The Roman City map is our favourite, however, brilliantly evoking the grand structures of Assassin's Creed: Brotherhood. The map took five months to build and features massive structures like a chariot racing track and the Colosseum in its original form, as well as luxury villas and lovely gardens. Run, climb and vault to your heart's content!

Ah, the famous Assassin's Creed guard. Totally expendable in every way. Don't any of these people have families?!

Let's just hope there's a lovely, soft bale of hay for Steve to land in. This is what we call a real leap of faith!

Fallout

Minecraft is already a survival game, so it only requires a tweak and some custom items to help make it suddenly feel like Fallout. Good resource packs and the Fallout mod do the job nicely.

Mineout Resource Pack

http://bit.ly/1k32oVi

Now we need to get Minecraft looking suitably disheveled, as though a thousand nuclear bombs have wiped out the world. The Mineout Resource Pack is a standout effort that retextures the world to make it look brown and filthy and unpleasant, in a good way!

The desert earth looks suitably desolate, NPCs now look like hardened wastelanders straight from Mad Max, and enemies have been redone to bring them closer to Fallout's mob. Cave spiders have been given a tail to turn them into radscorpions, while cows have received an extra face on their texture to turn them into the two-headed brahmin pack beasts of the wasteland. Also, chickens are green for some reason.

The inventory menu is especially neat. The mod adds a skin that makes it look as though you're equipping items using a Pip Boy. Or you can also have a go on the neat Industrial Wasteland Texture pack (http://bit.ly/1Nm2qPB), which looks more like Fallout: New Vegas.

Local Weather Mod

http://bit.ly/1uSaBxU

The Local Weather Mod adds some truly spectacular weather that will make your wasteland seem that bit more dangerous. Stormy!

You can't find a glass of clean drinking water, but giant robot helpers are everywhere. What a world!

Best of the rest

No matter what the genre, hundreds of classic game worlds have been remade in Minecraft. It goes to show that you can do almost anything with the will and a lot of time in creative mode.

CivilizationCraft

http://bit.ly/1Y1coQX

An interesting twist on the PC empire building strategy series, Civilization, this modded server asks players to band together to gather resources and create buildings that boost your empire. Those of course include some of Civ's famous wonders of the ancient world. It's a multiplayer affair that relies on trade, deal-making and competitive expansion. The buildings also look lovely, but be warned, "this is a very long term game" according to the CivilizationCraft wiki, that may require quite a lot of dedication if you're to get the most out of it.

Mine 4 Dead

http://bit.ly/1L1YkO8

A great co-op adventure map that pits you against zombie hordes in a doomed city. It honours the terrific zombie survival shooter with character textures representing every hero from the series. Safe rooms with beds offer brief respite, and there's even a four-minute finale event to mimic the desperate last stand moments of Left 4 Dead.

BioShock

http://bit.ly/1upB6bH

The city of Rapture is one of the best game worlds ever created, and now you get to explore it in block-based form thanks to this ambitious build.

MINECRAFT
MASTERMIND

How much do you really know about your favourite game?

Let's be honest: even your nanna could probably identify a creeper by now. "Is it that scuttly green thing, dear? Ooh, I don't care for him. Best make sure he doesn't go boom." Of course, if you consider yourself to be a Minecraft devotee, your knowledge should probably go a few blocks deeper than that. So take our quiz, and test your trivia smarts...

01 **What is the name of this block?**
A) Redstone
B) Glowstone
C) Cobblestone

02 **Which of these materials is the hardest?**
A) Iron
B) Gold
C) Obsidian

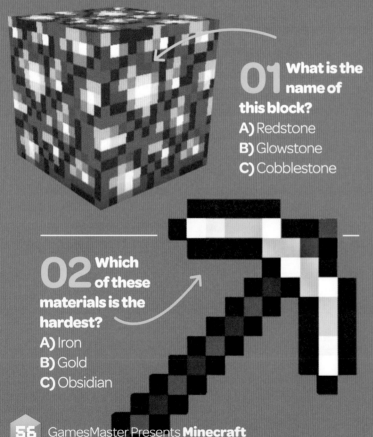

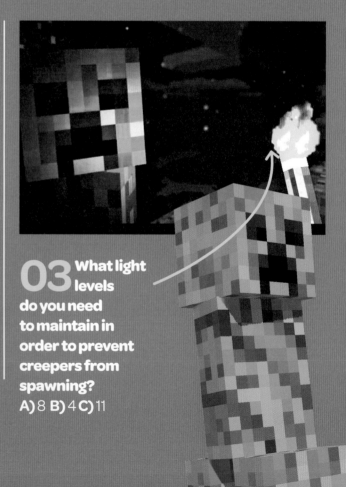

03 **What light levels do you need to maintain in order to prevent creepers from spawning?**
A) 8 B) 4 C) 11

04 How many adjacent blocks can be powered by one block of redstone?

A) 4
B) 2
C) 1

05 How many biomes are there in total?

A) 22
B) 10
C) 16

06 What do you get if you cross a cow and toadstool?

A) Mooshroom
B) Killer bunny
C) Nightmares

07 In what year was the first alpha version of Minecraft released?

A) 2001
B) 2009
C) 2011

08 How many platforms has Minecraft been released on in total?

A) 14
B) 8
C) 12

09 What is the name of the female player character?

A) Joanne
B) Stevena
C) Alex

10 What is the missing ingredient in this cake recipe: sugar, egg, wheat…?
A) Flour
B) Water
C) Milk

11 What is Minecraft creator Notch's real name?
A) Markus Persson
B) Jens Bergensten
C) Daniel Frisk

12 What is the name of the infamous 'ghost' (who does not exist) that some people have claimed to see in Minecraft?
A) Zerowine **B)** Herobrine **C)** Spectral Gary

13 Which British politician was recently turned into a Minecraft character?
A) David Cameron
B) Ed Miliband
C) Boris Johnson

16 How many items can you fit in a single chest?
A) 25
B) 27
C) 32

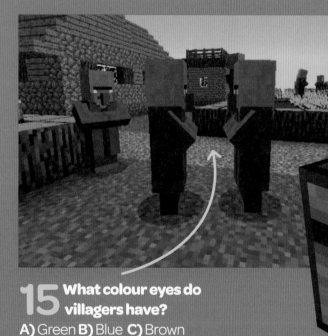

14 Where would you find a zombie pigman?
A) Forest biome
B) The Nether
C) The End

15 What colour eyes do villagers have?
A) Green **B)** Blue **C)** Brown

17 **What kind of mobs are squid?**

A) Hostile
B) Passive
C) Neutral

18 **Which of these will not stop an enderman from attacking you?**

A) Not looking at them
B) Wearing a jack o'lantern
C) Standing still while staring at them

19 **Which of these is the most sensible weapon against the Ender Dragon?**

A) Bow and arrows B) Sword C) Axe

20 **What was Minecraft's original title?**

A) Block Digger B) Cave Game
C) Special Steve's Subterranean Adventure

ANSWERS

01: B	09: C	17: B
02: C	10: C	18: C
03: A	11: A	19: A
04: A	12: B	20: B
05: C	13: C	
06: A	14: B	
07: B	15: A	
08: A	16: B	

RESULTS

0-5: Skeleton

Not many Minecraft facts in your mind, are there? Must try harder!

6-10: Villager

You know the lay of the land, but you're not the most adventurous.

11-15: Creeper

You may not be the main man, but you still pack an explosive punch.

16-20: Steve

Top of the blocks. You know the game inside out – well done!

CREEPER FACE BEANIE
Keep your bonce snug this

ENDERMAN SOFT TOY
There are loads of cuddly toys to buy. Just don't look this one in the eye...

MERCHCRAFT
Some of the very best Minecraft loot out now

MIGHT MINI FIGURES
These tiny figures are awesome for two reasons: 1) They're blind boxes, so you don't know which one you'll get and 2) You don't need loads of space to collect them!

DIGGING WALL DECAL
To add to that bedroom/mineshaft feel, this wall sticker makes it look like you're digging into your own wall. Amazing!

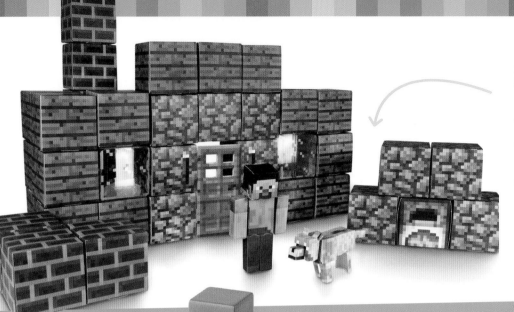

PAPER CRAFT SHELTER PACK

Want somewhere for all of your figures to live? These easy-to-build papercraft blocks are made from card, with clear folding instructions, so you won't be left frustrated.

CREEPER ANATOMY ZIP-UP JUMPER

Now you can be a Creeper inside and out! If that's what you've always wanted?!

ALEX FIGURE

With Steve merchandise being so easy to find, it's great to have a figure of his counterpart Alex to go adventuring with.

LEGO MINECRAFT THE MINE

If you want to really splash out, THIS is the way to go. The detail in this LEGO Mine set is just incredible.

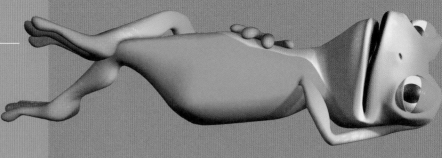

10

Minecraft PC passes to Beta development stage

Minecraft entered beta at the end of 2010, starting a period of development that added huge features to every aspect of the game. In beta, survival mechanics were expanded to include food and starvation, critical hits were added to combat, and you could gain experience for fighting monsters. New lighting systems and new graphical effects were added, beds let you skip night-time and reset your spawn point.

9

Notch quits Jalbum. net to work on Minecraft full time

In the early days of Minecraft's development, before it was clear the game would be a success, Notch was working at a photo gallery software company: Jalbum.net. However, after nine months there, it was clear Minecraft was a success, and Notch was earning far more from the game then he was from his salary. It was time to commit fully to his game. Notch didn't leave alone, though. Carl Manneh, Jalbum's CEO left with him too.

8

First demo released on TIGSource

On 17 May, 2009, 04:24:07 AM, Notch posted the first demo of what would become Minecraft. It was version 0.11a and was the barest essentials of the sprawling sandbox we know today. You could explore a procedurally generating landscape and you could break up blocks with your hands. Players could dig down into the vast caverns that littered the world. They could harvest blocks and replace them. Within 24 hours the thread had spawned more than three pages of responses. Features were suggested, criticism was offered, and screenshots were shared.

7

Mojang AB is founded

▶ Markus 'Notch' Persson and Jakob Porsér set up Mojang Specifications (now Mojang AB) in May 2009. The two had been friends for years, and soon brought in chum Carl Manneh as CEO. While the Stockholm-based company started out small, it now employs around 50 staff – and had racked up revenues of $80 million even by early 2012. Annoying for every mum who said videogames would never pay!

The Mojang team rocking some snazzy creeper shirts, before Markus Persson, Carl Manneh and Jakob Porsér left.

6

The creation of creepers

▶ Creepers are definitely Minecraft's most iconic mob, and we've already established that being blown up by one is a memorable moment in its own right. But did you know that they were originally a mistake? Notch didn't use modelling software to create Minecraft's creatures. Instead, he just wrote them in code. While trying to create a pig, he accidentally reversed the values for length and height. Instead of short and long, the resulting creature was tall and thin with four tiny feet.

Hiding among the cacti! That's a sneaky trick, even for creepers...

5
First ever Minecon

Minecon debuted in 2010 as MinecraftCon in Bellevue, Washington. Unlike the big Vegas and Disneyland events to follow, this first gathering was a small, informal affair. Visitors faced off over in-game rounds of Spleef – a race to destroy the blocks under your opponent – and threw a building competition, while Notch wandered around, meeting fans. The growth of Minecon from this humble starting point reflects Minecraft's explosion into mainstream popularity.

4
First Minecraft video on YouTube

Minecraft and YouTube go together like jelly and ice cream, or creepers and unprotected houses. Videos of the blocky wonderland have totalled 63 billion views – that's nearly ten views for every person on this planet. But the first ever YouTube video of Minecraft was posted by Notch and simply shows a cave (youtube.com/watch?v=F9t3FREAZ-k&feature=plcp). Ah, such innocence.

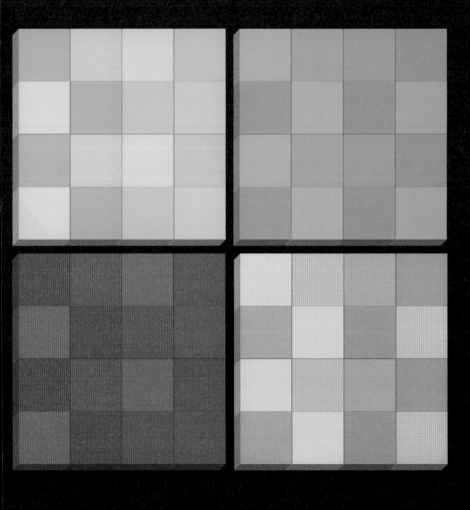

3
Microsoft buyout

On 15 September 2014, Microsoft paid $2.5 BILLION to buy Mojang and take control of Minecraft's future. At first, it seemed incredible anyone would want to pay that much for a game.However, with plans for a movie, merch, and new releases, it's almost certain that Microsoft will get its money back.

And and it's clear the game will play a large part in Microsoft's forthcoming HoloLens hardware.

2

Official version of Minecraft released

▶ Minecraft 1.0 was officially released on 18 November, 2011 during Minecon. Notch announced the launch on stage during his keynote address. The grand 1.0 update added The End dimension, new nether bricks, achievements, a hardcore mode, villagers, mushrooms and more. Animal breeding, potions and improved armour helped rebalance the game, and the 1.0 release fixed a bunch of bugs.

The release was a climactic moment, and the result of two-and-a-half years of busy development.

It's almost impossible to imagine the world before Minecraft

1 Notch leaves Mojang

▶ It started with a cold. In June, 2014, while laid up in bed with the flu, Notch started to receive angry messages on Twitter – a lot of angry messages. Minecraft players were annoyed about changes to the game's EULA (see page 9), and how servers were monetised. Changes, Notch says, he had nothing to do with. It was the last straw.

The anger directed at him for something he wasn't part of forced Notch to realise he didn't have the connection to his fans he thought he had. He didn't like it.

Notch reached out to Microsoft, and in September, 2014 wrote: "I'm not an entrepreneur. I'm not a CEO. I'm a nerdy computer programmer who likes to have opinions on Twitter."

TRAVEL FASTER

Using water in mob farms can make things easier, but if you put ice underneath the water you'll make things travel even faster.

FLAME PROOF

Wooden planks catch fire easily, but wooden slabs don't. If there's lava nearby and you don't have any cobblestone try using slabs instead.

ULTIMATE SURVIVAL TIPS!

Quick tips to give you the edge in survival mode

MINE SMARTER

Need to clear loads of sand or gravel but your spade is about to break? Use a torch to burn through a pile instead. Simply knock out the bottom block then quickly place a torch underneath and it will break the whole stack in seconds.

TAKE A BREATHER

Not sure how to explore underwater to see those Ocean Monuments without drowning? Take loads of ladders or signs with you – you can use them to make air pockets to catch your breath during long dives. Guardian fights here we come!

DON'T END UP LIKE ME!!!

THE GOLDEN RULE

Always take a chest with you when you're exploring. You don't want to lose all of those items you've spend so long collecting – better keep them safe just incase a stray skeleton arrow takes you down.

HOLD IT IN

Weirdly pressure plates can be used to hold in blocks of lava or water, even if you step on them – great for decorating or when you're trying to clear a safe path in a mine.

A to Z
MINECRAFT

Going back to school with the ABCs of Minecraft

A to Z

"ABC, it's easy as punching trees." Okay, so that's not really how the song goes, but let us dream/misquote – because we're bringing you a complete alphabet of Minecraft in all its glory.

Minecraft's all about the basics, you see: the building blocks, if you'll pardon the pun. Whether you're going for broke in Hardcore Survival mode or creating a 200-block-high portrait of your cat, building upon a solid foundation is vital.

Step away from that sandy biome, then, and let's take it back to the basics. The very basics. In just 26 letters...

A

APPLE

▶ A is always for apple in alphabets, isn't it? Well, the humble fruit isn't so basic in Minecraft. Its mystical powers don't stop at "can be shoved into your pie-hole to restore four food points". They're also a great way to bribe horses into giving free rides, the key to making the super-secret Mojang banner, and like everything, extra-delectable when dipped in gold.

B

BLOCK

▶ Biomes, buckets and blazes are all very well, but blocks are literally the stuff that Minecraft's made of. Other games sweated over making hyper-realistic worlds; Minecraft gave us square pumpkins, put on a sweet pair of shades and told us to deal with it. Plus, each in-game world is bigger than some planets in terms of in-game metres. Crazy, eh?

C

CREATIVITY

▶ There's only one thing about Minecraft beginning with the letter C that's worth mentioning. That'd be *creativity* of course. Minecraft's free-roaming, resource-stuffed Creative Mode has prompted works of art: reconstructions of Game of Thrones' Westeros; working computers; a playable guitar... there really are no limits!

D DIAMONDS

▶ Ah, diamonds. Light of our lives, fire of our torches, object of all our late-night mining sessions. Why do we players worship them so? Is it because they make the strongest, most efficient gear? Perhaps. Is it because crafting an Enchantment Table is impossible without them? Almost certainly.

E ERROR

▶ You can't have Minecraft without failure. In fact, if you're not regularly failing at Minecraft, you're doing it wrong. Every grisly death, misplaced pickaxe, wasted resource and accidental base bonfire is a step in the right direction. All the best stuff comes from mistakes. Even the creeper itself was a coding error.

GHAST

▶ Minecraft's most weird and wonderful mob just had to have its very own place in our A-to-Z. There's so much to know and love – well, tolerate – about the demon jellyfish ghost. Oh, you thought the Ender Dragon was king of the mobs? Ghasts are *even bigger* by volume. Their childlike gurgling/cooing/screaming is shudder-inducing...

F FRIENDS

▶ There's many a thrill to be had playing Minecraft in single-player mode. But multiplayer Minecraft is even better. Whether it's surviving the Nether together with friends, or constructing an elaborate free-running map to race, a little company goes a long way when you're off in search of fame and the Farlands.

HOUSE-KEEPING

▶ Hurried first-night dirt bunkers aside, crafting the perfect base is one of the greatest bits of playing the game. There are some truly epic specimens online: huge fortresses; sleek modern pads; cosy alpine lodges; whole skyscrapers filled with apartments. With gorgeous texture packs and detailed furniture mods, staying in is the new going out in Minecraft.

JUKEBOX

▶ Enter the jukebox, Minecraft's resident quadratic DJ, with sick beatz for all and a heart of diamond. Yes, of *diamond*, not gold. The music discs it plays can be found in dungeons chests, or dropped in the happy (yet rare) event of a creeper getting skewered by a skeleton's arrow.

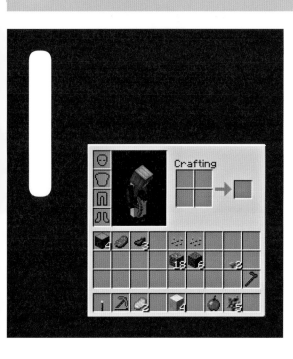

INVENTORY

▶ Your Minecraft inventory says a lot about you. We spend so much time staring at those neat little rows of grey boxes that it's left a permanent gridded overlay on our vision. Taking inventory is such an essential experience that you even get an achievement the first time you open it. Soon, it's your best friend: holding all your important tools and tidbits; waiting patiently as you eject all and sundry to make room for new loot.

KILLING

▶ All together now: it's the ciiiircle of liiiife... Killing is sort of essential in Minecraft's Survival mode. It's them or us, after all. At least it's sort of humane, as conquered creepers and crawlers disappear in a puff of smoke, XP and lovely, lovely loot.

L LEGO

▶ Everybody's favourite plastic stickybricks were most likely the unintentional inspiration behind Minecraft. Notch himself has a sneaking suspicion that his childhood stash of LEGO influenced him to create a blocky game about, well, creating. And we're just going to throw this out there: Minecraft is *better* than LEGO. It just is.

M MODDING

▶ Booting up mods via ModLoader or Forge totally changes your game. Sample thousands of new, exotic foodstuffs; explore hundreds of fantastical biomes; marvel at the majestic sight of an entire farm of exploding chickens. You can even alter or add in entire game mechanics.

O OCEAN

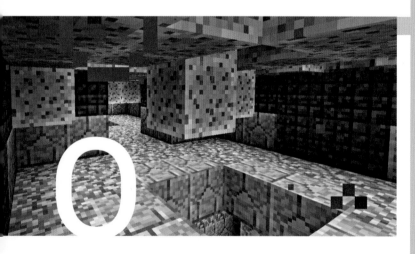

▶ The cavernous depths hide the most unbelievable secrets. The blue biome is an infinite source of delish fish for those savvy enough to rustle up a fishing rod, and zipping around its azure surface in a wooden boat is a pleasant diversion.

NOTCH

▶ Markus 'Notch' Persson is the man who created Minecraft, and he actually started making videogames from the tender age of eight. It may not surprise you, then, to learn that the loveable, fedora-clad meatball is actually a part of the Swedish branch of Mensa. (The gang for smart folk). Perhaps if we play enough, we'll get in too!

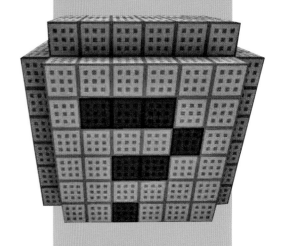

P

PIG

▶ Behold, the golden rule of Minecraft (and of life): when in doubt, bacon. Just the goofy expressions on the faces of these pixelated porkers can get you through the hard times. When a creeper lays waste to the labour of love that *was* your redstone auto-farm, solace arrives in the form of some light-hearted piggybacking. A saddle, a stick, some string and a tasty carrot later, you've got yourself a regular rodeo.

REDSTONE

R

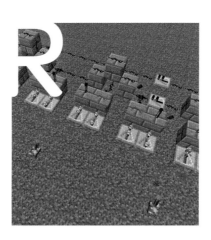

▶ So you've just seen a player press a button and automatically farm a whole field of wheat like it ain't even a thing. Magic! Sorcery! Calm down, it's just redstone. Epic minecart rollercoasters stretching on for miles, machines that can farm and fire arrows. It's all possible with redstone...

S

STEVE

▶ He's a man of few words, our Steve – and by few, we mean none. But don't be fooled by his lovely face: the stats suggest that Steve's actually some sort of terrifying demi-god. Not only can he *fly* in Creative mode, his casual walking pace is a blistering 9.7mph. Good grief, Steven, don't you ever stop to smell the roses?

Q

QUIZ

Heads up off your desks, Minecraft scholars. We're quite a way into our alphabet here, so let's check you've been paying attention.

Question 1 What S is a useful item that lets you block enemy attacks?

Question 2 What C is a type of block that ghosts can't destroy?

Question 3 What E speaks English backwards?

Question 4 What D is essential for a jukebox?

Question 5 What G can be found in ocean monuments?

Answers 1. Shield 2. Cobblestone 3. Enderman 4. Diamond 5. Guardian

TORCH

▶ Minecraft's wonderful torches have saved our custom skins on more than several occasions. Got lost on a jaunt away from your base and now the inky darkness of night-time is upon you? Torch. Mobs spawning on your roof and plopping down your chimney? Torch. Exploring the ocean and running out of oxygen? Potion of Water Breathing. Only joking, that stuff's expensive. TORCH.

UNDERGROUND

▶ You can go several Minecraft days, if not *weeks* without seeing the light of day – and that's just how we like it. Each cavern and winding tunnels must be combed for exposed ore; each lava lake doused in our efforts to mine obsidian; each ravine explored for an entrance to abandoned mineshafts.

VISTA

▶ It's all too easy to miss out on the little things. It's astonishing that a world composed entirely of 1x1 blocks can randomly generate such sublime horizons. Each corner you round can confront you with new stunning landmarks to gaze at.

WEATHER

▶ The forecast's clear and sunny by default, and you can toggle rain and snow on and off with a simple "/ weather rain" command, which would certainly come in handy in real life.

But things really kick off when it gets stormy The lightning's the worst: everything it strikes, it sets on fire... even you, to five hearts of damage.

X MARKS THE SPOT

▶ What good is a map without a lovely, fat, juicy X to encourage you to hunt something shiny? If you've got a predilection for piracy, searching for treasure with your pals is a brilliant way to raise the stakes. Thanks to maps and server plug-ins, it's possible to follow clues to find hoards of jewels and hidden gold.

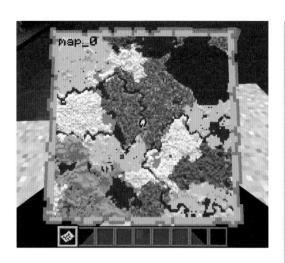

YOUTUBE

▶ One thing's for sure: Minecraft wouldn't be the worldwide phenomenon it is today without the power of the Internet, and specifically video-hosting website YouTube. Stampylonghead, Sky, CaptainSparkles, iBallisticSquid, iHasCupcake… No, we're not spouting nonsense – these are just some of the usernames of the world's biggest YouTubers who've shown the world, through their own unique brands, why Minecraft is so much fun. We love 'em, and Minecraft sure wouldn't be the same without them.

ZOMBIE

▶ Finally, bringing up the rear as usual, shambles in the zombie. The reason you never see a zombie in a stylish pair of specs? They've got the best eyesight in the game. They'll spot you from 40 blocks away, compared to other mobs squinting at your wobbly knees from just 16 blocks. Beware!

QUICK BUILD!

Set sail in this easy mini boat build...

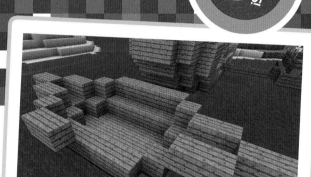

5 MINUTES!

START HERE!

1 START with this template at water level. It's five blocks long and one wide. Use any type of wooden plank you like.

2 FAN out the shape from the bottom to step away from the middle. You'll need two layers, but extend the ends a block.

BUILD THIS!

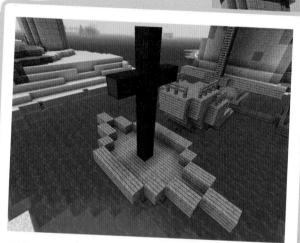

3 BUILD a mast nine blocks high out of a different wood type. Add some prongs sticking out at the seventh block.

4 ADD a sail using wool. To make it look like there's wind, step it one block forward. And now you're done!

HOW MANY PIGS AT THE MARKET CAN YOU SPOT?

It's a piggy-fest! But how many can you see below?

A LESSER-SPOTTED PIG

SEE HOW MANY YOU CAN FIND IN THIS SCENE!

EVERYBODY Loves our Minecraft-flavoured piggy pals. But can you spot them from a distance? To test your bacon detection skills, we've hidden a ham load in the picture above – but just how many? Write your answer down!

YAY! I DID IT! I COUNTED:

PIGS

WRITE YOUR ANSWER HERE...

MAKING MINECRAFT MUSIC WITH
CAPTAINSPARKLEZ

Jordan Maron doesn't just play Minecraft, he writes sweet, sweet music about it too. His blockbuster music videos feature slick animation, slapstick antics, and toe-tapping tunes, and they all take place in a world of colourful cubes.

NAME:
JORDAN MARON

SUBSCRIBERS:
9,472,971

CALLS FANS:
DUDES

MOST VIEWED VIDEO:
REVENGE: A MINECRAFT
ORIGINAL MUSIC VIDEO
– 163,274,819 VIEWS

CATCHPHRASE:
[DRAMATIC VOICE]
IN A WORLD WHERE...

SEARCHIN'

JORDAN'S most popular music video is the story of one Minecrafter's underground search for glittering diamonds. Our intrepid miner is working so hard that he doesn't realise the sun's gone down.

EXTRA ADVENTURES!

1 JORDAN also posts videos of his scraps in The Hunger Games arena. Here's the time he clinched victory in a 25-player match.

2 NOW he might be best known for his own tunes, but Jordan does funny parodies too, including a blocky version of Gangnam Styl

SHOCK TREATMENT

HERE'S the moment when our hero is rudely interrupted by an explosive Creeper! He gets one heck of a fright, but he manages to run away and scramble to the surface.

DON'T STAND SO CLOSE

EVERYTHING seems fine, until our hero turns around to see a horribly familiar face. This time, he doesn't even have time to run for cover before the green-skinned meanie explodes!

YOU CRAZY DIAMOND

THE singed miner is determined to get his revenge, and uses his astounding crafting skills to forge some shiny diamond armour and a powerful diamond sword.

SLICE AND EASY

AND then our intrepid mining hero finally takes his revenge on all those creepy Creepers in an epic sword-swinging showdown of truly cinematic proportions. It looks amazing!

We got one of these invitations too! What the heck is going on here?

3 JORDAN provided the voice for a character in Minecraft: Story Mode. Here he is playing it, with his character in the background.

4 SOMETIMES Jordan hops into custom Minecraft maps for a let's play video. Here he's fleeing a swarm of Nether Chickens!

MOUNTAIN CASTLE

DIFFICULTY: MEDIUM
TIME NEEDED: 40-60 MINS
EXTRA INFO: TRY USING DIFFERENT TEXTURE PACKS OR SKINS TO VARY THE LOOK

KING OF THE CASTLES!

Become royalty by building your very own stone fortress!

1

PICK YOUR PEAK

FIRST you'll need to find yourself a **tall mountain** – the kind that will be great for spotting enemies from. Pick one that you think has a **cool shape**, and preferably a flat bit to start building out from.

2

LAY YOUR FOUNDATIONS

CHOOSE the steepest outward facing side of the mountain and start **blocking out** the space for a sheer, narrow wall that lines up with the top of the mountain. Try to work in a **nice view**, too.

3

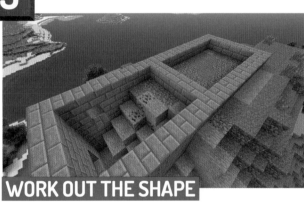

WORK OUT THE SHAPE

BLOCK out an area along the **top of the mountain** that will end up being your main room. Just build in the **outside bits** for now – you can do inside later once you've got your walls sorted.

4

TOWER BLOCK

START putting a **really tall tower** in place that goes up from your cliff wall. By putting it here it looks like it's extra tall and growing from the very mountain itself. It'll feel **more imposing** that way.

INSPIRATION

BRIDGE We love the way Origamiboy231 has joined the peaks with a stone bridge.

VINES The vines that hang by Clause925's fortress make it feel like it's near a forest.

WALLS Ytterbium70's huge wall is great for protecting the castle from outsiders.

5

BRICK IT OUT

FILL in the outside edges of your tower with **stone bricks**, leaving space for windows all the way up. You could always use **cobblestone** or any other kinds of bulding materials if you prefer.

6

CRAFT THE PARAPETS

AT THE very **top of your tower** it's time to add some parapets for decoration, and to make it look a bit more castley. Build a **ring of stone bricks**, and then use stairs in each of the corners.

7

BUILD AN EXTENSION

NOW it's time for you to **build out the hall** area. Make space for one floor from the area you marked out in Step 3 and fill it in with **stone bricks** or cobblestone just like you did with the tower.

8

WINDOWS AND DOORS

TIME to fill in all of those gaps with **windows and doors** to make it all look a bit more substantial! Add **glass panes** in each gap, but make a space for doors on top of your hall area.

9

ADD SOME BALCONIES

TURN the top of the hall into a **mega balcony** by adding a stone fence and a parapet pattern with stairs in each of the corners. You can also add a **small balcony** near the bottom of the tower.

10

ADD SOME FLOURISHES

NOW go back and add a little **detailing** to your walls – we're using cracked stones and **mossy stones** here and there to make it look less flat, but you may have your own decorating ideas.

11

SPREAD OUT

IT'S time to expand your pile! Pick a **different side** of the mountain that's underneath your tower – this will be your **town area**. Start blocking out sections from the mountain face.

12

MAKE A TOWN

ADD windows and doors at **different levels** of your buildings to make it feel like there's lots of small buildings **cobbled together**. That way it looks more natural and organic as a settlement.

13

BUILD A STAIRCASE

NOW you need stairs from the top tower to your town area. You can even **add another house** into the stairs themselves to act as some kind of a gatehouse – just like you get in **a real castle**.

INSPIRATION

CASCADE Noxus Bulgar's build feels like it fits right into that beautiful mountain.

FLOATING Lemon Fox goes one better by making a sky island with an airship dock.

EXOTIC Lumos's build goes for more of a tropical feel than the usual cold hills.

14

FINISH IT OFF

AND you're done! You can keep building on different areas of your mountain to add to the fortress feel. Or try switching to the **Fantasy texture pack** for a more authentic look.

Make it!
TASTY PIG SANDWICH BENTO

EAT ME WITHIN NICE BREAD!

Tasty eating fun with your favourite pink porkers. Vegetarians look away now!

INGREDIENTS

Bread, butter, ham (or Quorn ham slices), nori, cucumber, salad leaves, spring onion, feta cheese.

IF YOU LOVE YOUR PORCINE PALS, TRY QUORN SLICES INSTEAD.

1 SARNIE

Make your sandwich. We opted to fill ours with ham (it seemed only fitting) but you could use anything you like – just don't make it too thick. Buttering the bread will help the sandwich to stick together once you've packed it. Make sure that you butter the top slice of bread on both sides too for extra porky stickability.

INFO

PIG SANDWICH BENTO

DIFFICULTY: MEDIUM LOW
TIME NEEDED: 25 MINUTES
TELL MUM? IF YOU'RE USING SHARP KNIVES TO CUT STUFF!

MAKE A FACE

Remove the crusts and cut it into neat squares. Then lay another slice of ham on top, and carefully trim the edges so that there's no overhang. Cut a small square of ham to pop on the middle of each sandwich – this will make your pig's delicious snout. Cut out smaller squares of nori for its nostrils, as well as another pair of nori squares to go above them to create each pig's eyes.

HOW TO MAKE A FAKE PIG FROM REAL PIG. KINDA WEIRD, HUH!

JEEPERS CREEPERS

Cut off a piece of cucumber to lunchbox height, then slice it in half lengthways. Being careful not to cut your fingers, cut out the outline of a Creeper (get an adult to do this if it's a bit too tricky!). Use a cocktail stick to take off the cucumber skin to give it eyes and a mouth.

CARVE OUT YOUR VERY OWN HISSING BEAST FROM TASTY CUCUMBER.

BOX THEM UP!

Assemble your bento. We used a two-piece stacking box for this – one layer for the sandwiches, and the other for the cucumber Creeper on a bed of salad leaves with spring onion and crumbled feta cheese. You could just as easily compile this in one box, though, and use whatever salad you like.

KEEP THE CREEPER AWAY FROM YOUR PIG OR CHAOS MIGHT ENSUE!

YOU'RE GONNA WISH YOU NEVER SPAWNED ME, PUNY HUMAN!

INCREDIBLE...

EVERYTHING YOU NEED TO KNOW ABOUT...
THE WITHER

From how to spawn it to how to kill it...

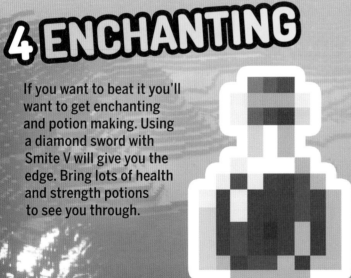

1 NETHER DATE

You'll need to head to the nether if you want to spawn a Wither. You'll need to gather Soul Sand, and then find a Nether Fortress to fight Wither Skeletons to harvest their skulls.

FIND THREE WITHER SKELETONS AND LOP OFF THEIR SKULLS!

2 PICK YOUR SPOT

Before you spawn it, you'll want to be as far away as possible from anything you hold dear. It will explode everything, including your perfectly crafted base, so only spawn it in areas you don't mind getting damaged. Being deep underground will limit its movements.

WITHERS ONLY ATTACK LIVING THINGS, NOT THE UNDEAD...

3 ENEMY OF MY ENEMY

The Wither will attack you, but it will also attack all other mobs except for the undead ones like zombies and skeletons. Mobs can make for useful distractions for you to get a few shots in.

4 ENCHANTING

If you want to beat it you'll want to get enchanting and potion making. Using a diamond sword with Smite V will give you the edge. Bring lots of health and strength potions to see you through.

5 GREAT REWARDS

If you kill it, you'll get a Nether Star which you can use to make a beacon – super handy for finding your way home after a long adventure.

FIVE GLASS AND THREE OBSIDIAN WILL TURN YOUR NETHER STAR INTO A BEACON!

5 FANTASTICAL BEASTS!
AND HOW TO MOD THEM!

Add a little animal magic to Minecraft

HOW TO INSTALL MINECRAFT MODS
Download Forge Modloader for your PC or Mac. Click the file to install. Then, download your mod (check the version of your mod matches your version of Forge). Drag the downloaded file into the mods folder of your game's Minecraft folder, and start playing!

There's plenty of life in Minecraft, from the cute and oh-so-harvestable mooshrooms, pigs and rabbits, to the slightly more problematic creepers, spiders and all the rest. It's alive with fur, legs and eyes (although not always in the best ratios) but it could be alive-er-er, which is a technical term for modding in extra hooves, claws and teeth. Step outside the vanilla menagerie and there's a range of interesting creatures just waiting to be tracked down or run away from, depending on what you've added.

This selection of extras will quite literally mod Minecraft to life. There's a wide range here with a variety of end results. You might simply want a few more creatures to cage and raise, or something more exotic to hunt. Maybe you fancy recreating Jurassic Park with some dinosaurs, or do you even want to make every creature ridable like a furry bike with feelings. There's something for everyone here, no matter how wild and unusual...

1 JURASSIC CRAFT 2.0.0

This is definitely one for the budding John Hammond's out there, and lets you add in a range of creatures that time forgot. All the big names are here, like Tyrannosaurus Rex, Velociraptors, Stegosaurus and, just because we want to hear you try and say it, Quetzalcoatlus. For super up to date fan service, even Jurassic World's completely-made-up Indominus Rex is in. There's a great range too from the classic options through to all the little bird-like missing links, giant prehistoric snakes and a range of water-based bitey things. The sense of scale is particularly impressive when you look up at a Brachiosaurus. Not only does it add loads of large lizards full of huge teeth (which as the films pointed out is generally a terrible idea) it expects you to create them the same way by harvesting fossils and amber to get DNA and then adding that to eggs to hatch your own pet dinos.
READ MORE: http://bit.ly/1tnrpwd

2 MUTANT CREATURES

T his doesn't add any new animals to Minecraft, it just make the regular ones far, far worse. It's all thanks to Chemical X which takes normal mobs and does horrible things to them. Throw it at the ground and it'll create a cloud of skulls that floats off in search of something to infect. It's not a guaranteed transformation though, with a 50/50 chance the potion will kill instead. However, assuming the creature lives, then it'll hulk out into a monsterised version of its former self. None of these changes are for the better: things like four-armed endermen, giant skeletons and a beefed up zombie with a ranged ground slam attack. Very little of this is a good idea. At least you can tame the spider-pig and ride it, instantly becoming the coolest kid ever.
READ MORE: http://bit.ly/1ZPYEGU

3 ANIMAL BIKES

O bviously the first rule of human/animal interaction is dominance. Mobs are there to do your bidding, and what better way to show nature who's boss than by turning every creature into a rideable mount. So here's the Animal Bikes mod which does just that. You'll need a saddle if you want to ride (craft one from three rawhide, one string and one iron bar), but once you're prepared it opens up a world of beast-based locomotion/cruelty. Not only can you belt around the world on just about any creature, but each has a special ability. So spiders climbs walls, cows can jump two blocks, pigs are fast and chickens flutter to the ground instead of falling. But it's better when you try the more fantastical offerings, like a My Little Pony lookalike that flies and leaves a trail of flowers. But you simply haven't lived until you've taken to the air on a fire breathing Ender Dragon. And to think, we were getting excited about making dinosaurs earlier.
READ MORE: http://bit.ly/1SWr2TE

4 MO' CREATURES

Mo' Creatures takes things a step further, sprinkling in a range of bigger, more interesting creatures, and, frankly, some hugely impractical extras. Two-headed, club-wielding ogres anyone? Yeah, who thought that was a good idea? Anyway, let's start with the less dangerous stuff. Well, slightly less dangerous at least: things like lions and crocodiles. There's definitely a more zoo-ey vibe added overall when you throw in ostriches, elephants and komodo dragons. It also leans slightly into fantasy land with those ogres we mentioned, giant scorpions and wyverns (think hipster dragons). Everything drops items like eggs, hides, chitin, claws and other materials that can be used for crafting the weapons and armour you'll need to stay alive. Crucially though, if you remember nothing else, remember this: the ostriches are ridable. Good luck going back to boring real life after you've done that...

READ MORE: http://bit.ly/1SWkHrB

5 CRAFTABLE ANIMALS

There's a horrible, nightmarish logic behind this mod – that if you get enough pork chops and smush them back together you can make a pig. Try not to think about that too much because there's a lot of fun to be had from the ability to remake creatures from bits. For starters, you can craft any animal in the game, like you would an item. On top of that you can armour your meat army, and create unique things like creeper jockeys, who ride proudly atop a spider, and giant versions of most mobs. There's a few interesting extras too, like the minimiser which switches things between adult and baby versions at will, a hologram display that will show off anything in the game at any scale, and the ace animal bow.

READ MORE: http://bit.ly/1XoJo16

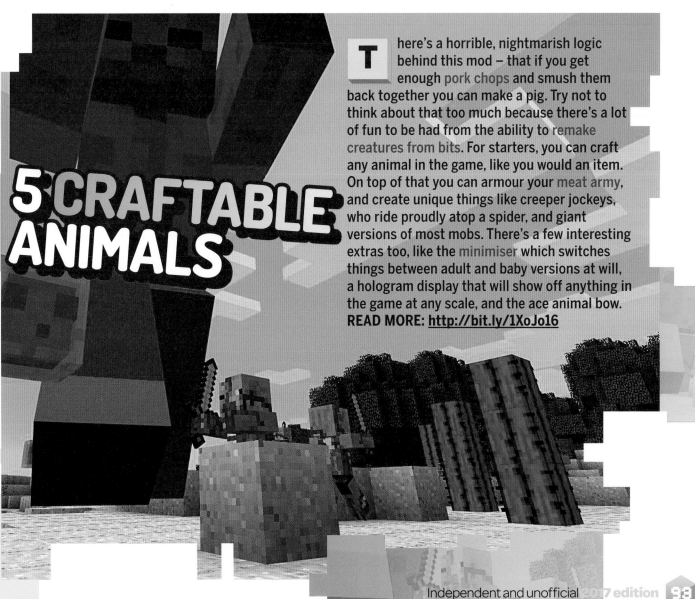